To my grandchildren
and all children everywhere . . .
–Mary Jo

ISBN 13: 978-1-4621-4435-8

Published by CFI, an imprint of Cedar Fort, Inc.
2373 W. 700 S., Suite 100, Springville, UT 84663
Distributed by Cedar Fort, Inc., www.cedarfort.com

Library of Congress Control Number: 2022950656

Cover design and interior layout by Shawnda T. Craig
Cover design © 2023 Cedar Fort, Inc.

Printed in China

10 9 8 7 6 5 4 3 2 1

Printed on acid-free paper

He is Jesus,
righteous and strong.
He helps me to know
the right from the wrong.

If I see a picture
that doesn't feel right,
the Savior can help me
get back to the light.

Jesus lived
a long time ago,

in a place far away
that I do not know.

He healed the sick
and raised the dead.

He listened
to God and did
what He said.

I want to follow
God too! I'll obey!

If I see a picture
that doesn't feel okay,
I will close my eyes.
I will turn away.

I can talk to God.
I can pray, pray, pray!

Now Jesus lives in
heaven above
and
sends me the Spirit
to fill me with love.

Jesus loves me.
He is real.
How do I know this?
I can feel . . .

Inside my heart,
my feelings know

the Savior loves me
head to toe.

He made the stars,
and sun, and sky,

and when things
happen, He knows why.

I love Him so much
my heart could burst.

He loves me when I'm good
and when I'm at my worst.

He wants me to be to safe and
keep peace and happiness first.

I trust Him and He trusts me
to become the person
I was meant to be.

I am trying to be kind.
I am trying to be good.
I am trying to watch
only things that I should.

If I see something on
a screen that makes
my heart feel strange,
I can turn it off.
I can rearrange.

I can tell people I trust.
Telling safe people
is a must!

I don't need to run, I don't need to hide.
Jesus will help me share what I'm
feeling inside.

I can tell the truth.
I can know what to say.
My troubled feelings can go away.

Some pictures are good, others are bad.
I can know the difference.
I can tell mom or dad.

Our Savior will help me.
His love is always true.

I can feel it in my heart,
and so can you!